Where Is Missouri?

Where Is Missouri?

by Annette Whipple

illustrated by Ted Hammond

Penguin Workshop

To all readers who celebrate curiosity—AW

PENGUIN WORKSHOP
An imprint of Penguin Random House LLC
1745 Broadway, New York, NY 10019
penguinrandomhouse.com

Designed and Produced by Dinardo Design, LLC.

Library of Congress Cataloging-in-Publication Data is available.

First published in the United States of America by Penguin Workshop, 2026

Manufactured in the United States of America
CJKW

ISBN 9798217243761 (paperback)
10 9 8 7 6 5 4 3 2 1

ISBN 9798217243778 (library binding)
10 9 8 7 6 5 4 3 2 1

The authorized representative in the EU for product safety and compliance is Penguin Random House Ireland, Morrison Chambers, 32 Nassau Street, Dublin D02 YH68, Ireland, https://eu-contact.penguin.ie.

Contents

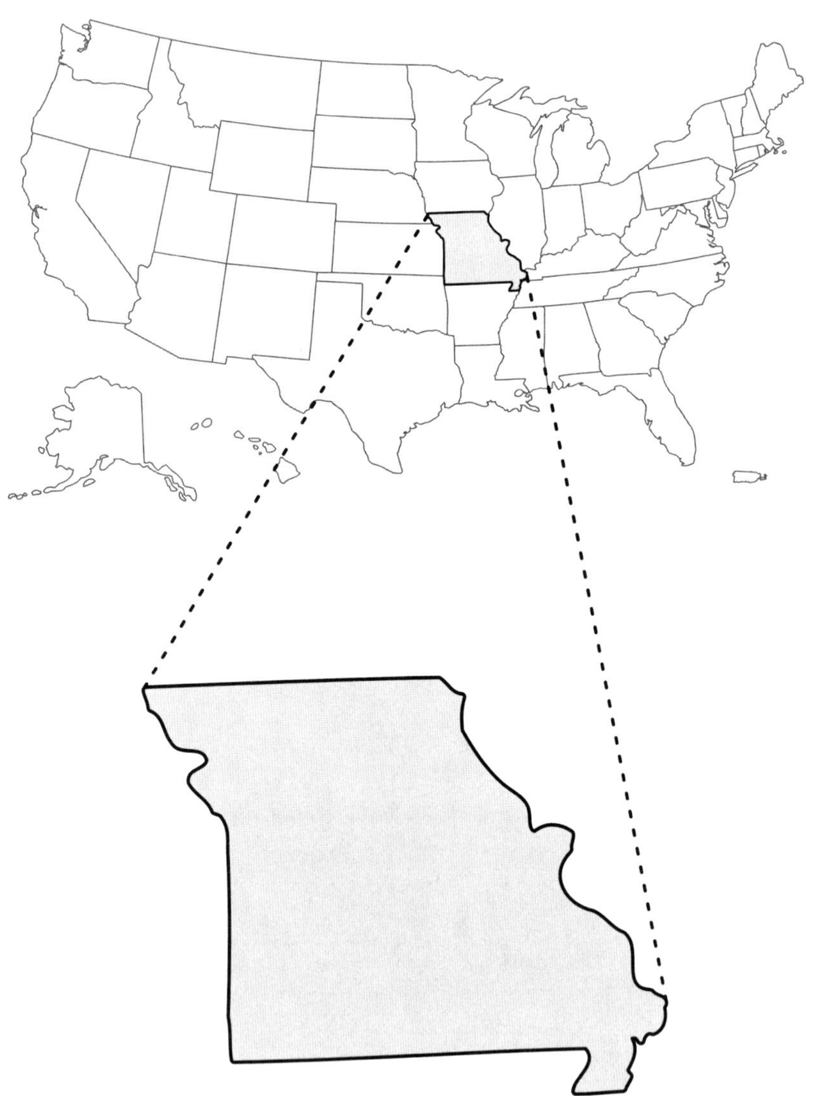

Where Is Missouri?

Crowds gathered in the streets of St. Joseph, Missouri, on April 3, 1860. They were waiting to witness the beginning of a new connection between their state and the far west coast of the United States.

When a cannon finally blasted, twenty-year-old Johnny Fry rushed through the streets on horseback. He crossed the Missouri River at the edge of town. He rode for eighty miles until he reached the next station on the Pony Express in Seneca, Kansas, and passed along the bag of mail he carried.

Fry had just completed the opening leg of the first-ever westbound Pony Express ride. In Seneca, a new rider took the mailbag packed with newspapers, telegrams, and letters and carried it to another station and another new rider. It took many riders and horses for the mailbag to make the journey to Sacramento, California, but they did it in just ten days!

The Pony Express was a way to speed up communication between the eastern and western parts of the country. This was before trains, roads, or even telegraph wires connected to the West Coast. Men and boys—one as young as eleven—raced on horseback through dust storms and blizzards to deliver mail. Missouri was a central point of the United States.

CHAPTER 1
Missouri and First People

Located near the middle of the country, Missouri is surrounded by eight states. Missouri includes a balance of urban centers as well as many farms in rural areas. It's known for industry (businesses and factories), agriculture (farming), and beautiful views.

This midwestern state covers nearly seventy thousand square miles. About one-third of it is covered by forests. The Missouri River flows through the middle of the state and meets up with the Mississippi River, which forms the state's eastern border.

The Ozarks are a heavily wooded area with hills covering much of the state. Large areas of flat lands with few trees called plains and prairies

are in the north. The southeastern corner of the state, called the Bootheel because of how it sticks out on a map, includes swamps and rich soil for farming. Throughout the state, the unique combination of hills, water, and limestone has formed more than 7,500 caves. The famous Bridal Cave is known for its stunning underground formations and educational tours. It's also where nearly five thousand weddings have occurred—underground!

Above ground, Missouri experiences four distinct seasons. Wet springs can bring flooding to local rivers and streams. Some summer days get hotter than one hundred degrees. Colorful leaves brighten Missouri's landscape during fall until the cold sets in for snowy winters.

Missouri's forests, plains, mountains, and rivers provide diverse habitats and homes for a wide variety of plants and animals. Nine-banded armadillos, river otters, and great blue herons live there. Nocturnal tiger salamanders and American bullfrogs live around streams and ponds. About eight inches in size, black-capped birds called interior least terns were once common near the Mississippi River. Forty years ago, they were listed as an endangered species. Scientists and others worked to protect their nests and habitats. The efforts have helped immensely. Interior least terns are no longer threatened!

People have also made homes in what is now Missouri for thousands of years. We don't know

what the earliest group called themselves, but historians call them the Mississippian people (they are also called Cahokians). About one thousand years ago, the Mississippian people built permanent villages. These villages included temples and observatories to watch the night sky. They also left behind huge mounds that were used for burials, religious ceremonies, and more.

The Mississippian people were the last major prehistoric (before written history) civilization on the continent north of Mexico. The location of

present-day St. Louis was near the center of that civilization. Mississippians built at least twenty-five mounds there. The largest one was the size of a football field and more than thirty-four feet high! Though most mounds have been destroyed, St. Louis still earned the nickname of Mound City.

The community and mounds of the Mississippian people were abandoned. The Cherokee, Chickasaw, Kanza, Missouria, and Osage (say: Oh-SAGE) Nations are some of the groups that are direct descendants of the Mississippian people.

The Osage people hunted, farmed, and gathered food from the land. Their homes could be as long as one hundred feet. This group claimed a lot of land and were known to be fierce fighters.

The Missouria people planted crops in the spring. They were seminomadic. That means they left their villages for long periods of time but then would return. Summer and late fall were spent away hunting bison, while spring and early fall were spent planting and harvesting. Later, the state was named for the Missouria Nation.

Everything changed for the Kanza, Chickasaw, and other Indigenous peoples, such as the Shawnee, in 1673 when a small group of French people led by Louis Jolliet went down the Mississippi River. These explorers claimed the land for France, even though there were already Indigenous people living there. France, Spain, and England all claimed the land of Missouri at different times in the late 1600s and 1700s.

The French established the first permanent village for European people in Missouri by 1750 and called it Ste. Geneviève (say: Saint JEN-uh-veeve). It had just twenty-three people in it. They farmed the land and collected salt from a spring. Soon, some miners came to Missouri to dig for a mineral called lead (say: LED). St. Louis became a trading post in 1763, and about the same time, Cape Girardeau (say: JUR-ard-oh) did, too. Fur trappers, settlers, and miners brought items, such as animal furs, to trade for goods. The furs were sent east or to Europe to be sold.

Some Indigenous nations also traded with the Europeans. Items such as guns, knives, blankets, beads, and furs were exchanged. Although some Indigenous people were killed while fighting with European settlers and other nations, many more were killed by illness. Europeans brought sicknesses with them. Smallpox was a deadly disease that the Indigenous peoples had never been exposed to before. It devastated them. The Missouria's population was about ten thousand in 1700. Over the next hundred years, it shrank to fewer than one thousand.

During this time, the United States of America was formed. Thirteen British colonies along the East Coast had rebelled and declared their independence from Britain in 1776. The war called the American Revolution ended in 1783. As European immigrants came to the new country, some moved to the land west of the Mississippi River.

At the time, what we now call Missouri was part of a huge area of land called Louisiana, and it was owned by France. The territory went from the Mississippi River all the way west to the Rocky Mountains and from Canada to New Orleans. The United States wanted the land. President Thomas Jefferson bought all of what was called Louisiana Territory for $15 million in 1803, in a deal called the Louisiana Purchase. It added 828,000 square miles to the country. The Louisiana Purchase doubled the size of the United States!

Jefferson thought if more settlers could own land and farm in the United States, the country would become more successful. He had a plan.

But first, he needed to know what the land was like between the Mississippi River and the Pacific Ocean. So, he hired Meriwether Lewis and William Clark to lead an expedition, or exploratory trip. A young Shoshone woman named Sacagawea was also a part of the expedition. She helped communicate with the Indigenous

nations they met along the way.

In 1804, the Lewis and Clark Expedition began near what is now St. Louis and went all the way to the Pacific Ocean, near what is now Astoria, Oregon. The group kept diaries, drew maps, and wrote notes about the land, plants, and animals. They found many species European settlers hadn't seen before, including nearly two hundred plants and more than one hundred different types of animals, such as the pronghorn antelope. The group also met more than fifty Indigenous nations. The explorers traded goods and gave leaders gifts, but they also told them that the United States now owned the land where these nations had always lived.

The explorers returned to Missouri with important information after traveling more than eight thousand miles in two years. The United States was about to change.

CHAPTER 2
Early Missouri

The US government had paid France for the land they acquired with the Louisiana Purchase, but they had not paid the Indigenous nations who lived on that land. The country used formal agreements, called treaties, to negotiate with Indigenous nations.

These treaties stated that nations such as the Osage would allow white settlers to use their land. In exchange, the government promised to leave the Indigenous nations' land alone so groups like the Osage could live and hunt. But the US government didn't keep their treaty promises. The Indigenous nations were repeatedly and violently forced to give up their land and move.

European settler communities grew, but they

also faced setbacks. The New Madrid earthquakes of 1811 to 1812 shook the land for several months. The rumblings were centered in New Madrid, Missouri, but they made church bells ring in Philadelphia and Boston. In addition to the tremendous shaking, there were landslides. The town of New Madrid was destroyed. Houses crumbled. Riverbanks washed away. New hills and valleys formed. The earthquakes even caused the Mississippi River to appear to flow backward temporarily! At the time, they were the strongest earthquakes to shake the United States and Canada east of the Rocky Mountains.

Missouri grew enough to become the twenty-fourth state on August 10, 1821. It was admitted to the United States as a state where slavery was legal. This was part of the Missouri Compromise. St. Louis and St. Charles were capitals before Jefferson City became the permanent capital in 1826.

The Missouri Compromise

As the population grew in Missouri Territory, the residents wanted it to officially become part of the United States. In 1818, the territory applied for statehood. Congress—the branch of the US government that makes laws—was concerned. At that time, the United States had eleven states that allowed slavery and eleven that did not. Congress wanted to keep that balance since the issue of whether or not slavery should be legal was already beginning to split the country. Congress denied Missouri statehood.

Soon, Maine applied to become a state. A congressman suggested both Maine and Missouri should be admitted. Maine would be a free state, and Missouri would be a slave state. The balance would be kept. The law became known as the Missouri Compromise. Part of this 1820 agreement

also said there would be no slavery allowed in future territories north of Missouri's southern border.

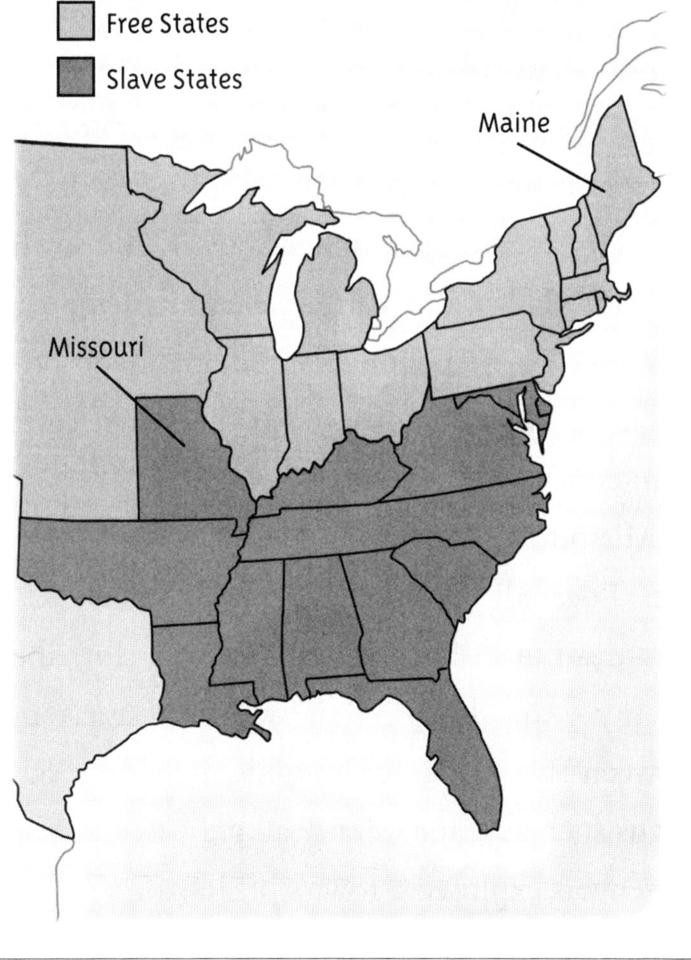

More people moved to Missouri. Many were farmers. Before planting in the Ozarks, farmers often had to clear the land. Some trees that were cut down were used to build log cabins. Often, they also brought seeds with them for their first crops. Many planted and grew the food they would need throughout the year, such as potatoes. They also grew crops such as corn, wheat, and oats. Horses and oxen pulled wagons and worked in fields. Hogs and cattle were raised for meat and milk. Some people planted apple and peach orchards. Most families made their own clothes from cotton they harvested.

Missouri's population increased. Towns spread out. Located on the Mississippi River, Cape Girardeau had been a trading post for about seventy years. In 1835, it was the busiest port between St. Louis and Memphis, Tennessee. River towns such as Cape Girardeau grew as steamboat passengers explored a town's businesses.

The rivers were great for business, but they were also home to mosquitoes. These insects carried a disease called malaria. They passed it to humans through their bites. Since mosquitoes like to live along streams and rivers, people in Missouri became extremely sick with malaria. Many people died. A farmer named John S. Sappington in Arrow Rock was also a doctor. He experimented with quinine, a medication from the bark of a South American tree used to treat malaria. He successfully created a quinine pill. Sappington's quinine pill soon became the

common malaria treatment in the Midwest.

Although many people wanted to explore these growing towns, not everyone who came through Missouri had chosen to be there. Many enslaved African people were brought to Missouri after it became a state and were forced to work for no pay and under terrible conditions. Thousands of Indigenous people also passed through the state in the 1830s after President Andrew Jackson passed a law called the Indian Removal Act. It said Indigenous people had to leave the eastern United States and move to Indian Territory (now called Oklahoma). The US Army forced thousands of Seminole, Cherokee, Creek, Chickasaw, and Choctaw people to march across several states, including Missouri. Many Indigenous people died on the journey. The path they took is now called the Trail of Tears.

Other people passed through Missouri by choice on long trips. They were pioneers, and they arrived with everything they owned in wagons. The Oregon Trail was the two-thousand-mile-long path that began in Independence, Missouri, and went west to Oregon. Groups of people—along with their livestock—migrated together in wagon trains, looking for land to claim and settle. One train included over one hundred wagons and one thousand people. This was part of a large expansion west for American settlers from the South and the East. Most pioneers began their journey with the Oregon Trail.

St. Louis quickly grew as people moved west and traveled up and down the river. The pioneers bought and traded food, animals, and necessary items to prepare for their five-month journey. St. Louis was the last place they could stock up on supplies before heading out on the Oregon Trail. Travelers needed wagon repairs, supplies, and boats, so it was a good place to set up a business. Most continued to their destinations, but some chose to stay in Missouri. The Oregon Trail became even more popular in the 1850s after gold was discovered in California, and St. Louis grew again. In 1803, at the time of the Louisiana Purchase, St. Louis had been home to about one thousand people. By 1860, more than 150,000 people lived there!

That same year, the Pony Express was set up to deliver mail from St. Joseph to Sacramento. This mail service linked the West Coast to the rest of the United States. The Pony Express employed more than two hundred riders and established about two hundred relay stations. Riders didn't stop until they'd gone about one

hundred miles. (On the Oregon Trail, wagons covered twenty miles a day—and they stopped for a midday meal.) The Pony Express was central to the country's communication, though it lasted only nineteen months before it was replaced by the telegraph. Whether letters or people were on the move, Missouri was officially the Gateway to the West.

Communication and business became easier when the railroad expanded into Missouri and westward. Missouri was becoming known as a state of progress. It offered transportation and manufacturing, as well as higher educational opportunities with the University of Missouri and William Jewell College.

Progress brought debates about slavery across Missouri in the 1800s. A man named Dred Scott was enslaved from birth but later lived in the free territories of Illinois and Wisconsin. Then Scott and his wife Harriet moved to Missouri. A law there said that once an enslaved person had lived in a free state, they couldn't be enslaved again. Dred and Harriet Scott decided to sue for their freedom in Missouri because the law seemed to be on their side. The case began in Missouri but made it to the US Supreme Court. A US Supreme Court justice said that people of African descent like the Scotts couldn't be citizens, or full members, of the United States. If they weren't citizens, then the law didn't apply to them. The Scotts lost the court case, which became known as the Dred Scott Decision.

With the Dred Scott Decision came even more disagreement and violence related to slavery. This led to the Civil War, beginning in 1861. The Union (Northern states) supported ending slavery, and the Confederacy (Southern states) wanted slavery to continue.

Would Missouri secede—or leave—the United States to join the Confederacy? The whole nation wanted to know which side Missouri would choose because the state had a lot to offer the war effort. Its many horses and mules would be important, as well as its rivers and railroads. St. Louis had machine shops and factories capable of making weapons. The nation stored gunpowder and muskets in a Missouri arsenal. There was enough there for an entire army! But which army would get it?

Missouri put the issue of leaving the Union to a vote. Though there were about one hundred thousand enslaved people in the state, Missouri chose to remain with the Union. Like the nation, the state was divided.

One of the first important land battles of the Civil War was in Boonville, Missouri. By the end of the war, over 1,200 battles had taken place in the state. About 110,000 Missouri men fought for the Union army, but at least 30,000 enlisted in the Confederate army. When the war ended in 1865, the Union prevailed, and slavery was outlawed in the United States. Everyone in Missouri finally had their freedom.

CHAPTER 3
The Making of Modern Missouri

After the Civil War, the state was still divided. A racist group formed called the Ku Klux Klan (KKK). White members of this group terrorized Black people of all ages. Still, many in Missouri were happy that slavery had finally been abolished, or ended. They were ready for peace.

Before the Civil War, it was illegal to teach Black people to read in Missouri. Reverend John Berry Meachum opened a school for Black students from Missouri anyway, on a steamboat anchored in the Mississippi River. This school was called the Floating Freedom School. The river was ruled by the federal government and not by the state, so it was legal to teach Black people to read there. After the war, all Black people in the United States had the legal right to read. More schools opened for Black students. Books, magazines, and newspapers also became easier to get in the late 1800s.

Mark Twain was a famous author who wrote stories set in Missouri, including *The Adventures of Tom Sawyer*. Twain was known for writing about life along the Mississippi River, as well as for his humor.

Missouri wanted to bring even more people to live in the state. Advertisements across the country promised rich soil and a climate that was "near perfect for health." Many people decided to move to Missouri, including Almanzo and Laura Ingalls Wilder. In 1894, they packed their covered wagon and traveled nearly seven hundred miles with their seven-year-old daughter from South Dakota to Mansfield. They bought forty acres of land, cleared it of trees, and farmed it. Laura wrote the Little House books from there.

With people such as the Wilders coming for farmland and others moving to the state's cities, Missouri grew. In 1890, St. Louis was the fourth-largest city in the nation, with almost half a million people living in it! It was a major manufacturing and transportation center. River and railroad access made it easy to transport products made in factories and on farms throughout the country.

St. Louis was making a name for itself. It wasn't just a gateway to the West—it was a tourist destination. More than twenty million visitors came to the city in 1904 when Missouri hosted the World's Fair, and more came the same year when St. Louis hosted the Summer Olympic Games.

Kansas City provided entertainment. In the 1920s, the neighborhood of 18th & Vine Streets was known as the Jazz District. Black musicians there helped develop this new style of music with complex rhythms and unplanned performances. Count Basie and Charlie Parker were two

Missourians who made jazz famous.

When the Great Depression hit the United States in 1929, there was little spare money for entertainment. During this period, many businesses and factories couldn't pay their employees. People lost their jobs and homes. Unemployment was especially high in St. Louis, where as many as five thousand people built temporary homes from wood scraps and garbage along the banks of the Mississippi River. They called their community Hooverville (named

after the unpopular president). They had their own mayor and even built a church from orange crates. As more work became available, many people returned to jobs and traditional homes.

Kansas City continued to appeal to visitors with its musicians, interesting architecture, community parks, and French roots. Some referred to the city as the Paris of the Plains. For decades, Missouri was the place to be for big musicians. In the very early 1900s, Scott Joplin blended Black music traditions along with classical music as a composer and pianist and was known as the King of Ragtime. Chuck Berry became one of the founding fathers of rock and roll, with strong guitar sounds and catchy lyrics in the 1950s. Tina Turner debuted as a rhythm and blues musician in the 1960s and continued to release albums for more than thirty years.

The country's tallest monument was completed in 1965. The St. Louis Gateway Arch

Tina Turner

stands 630 feet above the Mississippi River. Engineers designed the curving arch with over five thousand tons of steel and foundations sixty feet deep. It can be seen from thirty miles away!

Missourians also came to St. Louis to see baseball. Fans from all over Missouri celebrated when the St. Louis Cardinals competed against the Kansas City Royals in the 1985 World Series. The Royals secured the victory in seven games.

People also came together when tragedy

struck. The Great Flood of 1993 destroyed parts of Missouri when the Missouri River flooded. The Great Flood covered more than twenty million acres of land and flooded at least seventy-five towns in nine states. The state was devastated again when a tornado hit Joplin in 2011. More than one thousand people were injured, and 161 people died. Joplin came together to rebuild schools, homes, and hospitals.

Through the early 2000s, Missouri was not only rebuilding but also supporting transportation across America. The state manufactures equipment for land, water, and air travel with railroad cars, barges, and airplanes. In addition, the state produces dairy products, such as milk and ice cream, as well as chemical products, such as fertilizer and medicine, which are widely used across the country. Missouri remains a hub for transportation and for these important industries.

CHAPTER 4
Missouri Today

Today, some of Missouri's biggest employers include manufacturing, health care, and finance. Mining lead, zinc, and iron continues, with nearly six thousand mines in the state. Missouri produces 90 percent of the nation's lead and is second in the United States for lead production.

Agriculture is still a big business in the state. Only Texas has more farms. Soybeans and corn are two of Missouri's biggest crops. Cattle, turkeys, and hogs are some of its most common farm-raised animals. Missouri is also a global leader in agricultural technologies, which bring together science and research to support farming.

The state is home to many large corporations that began as small local businesses. Joyce C. Hall founded the Hallmark greeting card company as a teen in 1910. Now, Hallmark is one of the biggest card companies in the country. Johnny Morris sold fishing gear from the back of his father's store in 1972. Today, he encourages everyone to enjoy the outdoors through Bass Pro Shops and Cabela's stores throughout North America. In 1997, Maxine Clark founded Build-A-Bear Workshop. She now has four hundred stores around the world where customers can "build" a

stuffed animal. David L. Steward started World Wide Technologies in 1990. Based in St. Louis, today it is the largest Black-owned company in the country.

Missouri isn't just about business. Over forty-two million tourists visited Missouri in 2024. From big cities to mountain towns, the state has a lot to offer its visitors.

Millions of visitors go to Gateway Arch National Park each year. Some ride a tram to the top of the arch and explore nearly one hundred

acres in the park. Staff can use 1,076 steps on either side of the arch for maintenance or emergencies.

Missouri's state parks provide peaceful views and opportunities for outdoor recreation, such as golfing, hiking, and horseback riding. With fifty-seven state parks in total, there's something for everyone. Walkers, bikers, and horse riders all use the 240-mile-long rail-trail (a path created from a former railroad) at Katy Trail State Park. Lake of the Ozarks, one of the largest human-made lakes

in the country, offers 1,100 miles of shoreline to explore.

Kansas City is still known for the 18th & Vine district. Today, the district is rich in culture and entertainment. In addition to the shops, theaters, and restaurants in the district, a yearly festival showcases talented artists and musicians, bringing the community together.

Kansas City is also famous for its fountains. Long ago, fountains provided drinks to thirsty traveling animals. Today, children play in the Crown Center Square Fountain while visitors to the Henry Wollman Bloch (say: block) Fountain watch a water show every hour and a half. With more than two hundred fountains, the city features many of them in its community parks.

Visitors can try Missouri's famous barbequed meats. The state now has over one hundred BBQ restaurants. St. Louis barbecue usually has a lighter sauce, while Kansas City cooks use thick sauces.

Kansas City restaurants also made crusty scraps of brisket (a kind of beef), called burnt ends, a menu favorite. Missouri is also known for toasted ravioli (which is breaded and fried) as well as St. Louis–style pizza, which has a very thin crust and is cut into squares. It's not just the big cities with great food. Lambert's Cafe is home of "throwed rolls" with locations in Sikeston and Ozark. With each meal order, servers toss hot dinner rolls from across the room to customers, adding to the fun and casual atmosphere.

Along with great food and fun, Missourians have been passionate about sports for a long time. Players such as Willie Wells and Cool Papa Bell became famous with the St. Louis Stars, a Negro League professional baseball team. The league was created for Black players in 1920. The Negro Leagues Baseball Museum in Kansas City is dedicated to the talented athletes who weren't allowed to play in white professional leagues. Today, baseball fans root for the St. Louis Cardinals and the Kansas City Royals, while hockey fans cheer for the St. Louis Blues. Patrick Mahomes and Travis Kelce attract attention with the Kansas City Chiefs football team. The Chiefs won the 2023 and 2024 Super Bowl Championships!

Kansas City is known as the Soccer Capital of America. Men play for the Sporting Kansas City.

The Kansas City Current is the women's team. Their soccer stadium was the first one built for a women's professional team in the world. Kansas City is a host city of the 2026 World Cup, which is a global soccer championship. Teams from around the world compete in the tournament. Soccer is big throughout the state. Fans also cheer on the St. Louis City Soccer Club.

Missouri is also known for one of its natural

features: extreme weather! The state experiences tornadoes, earthquakes, and flooding. In 2024, more than one hundred tornadoes ripped through the state. Neighbors helped neighbors—and strangers—to rebuild. Earthquakes happen when huge slabs of rock move beneath Earth's surface. Scientists track about two hundred small earthquakes a year in Missouri—and most aren't even felt! Experts expect another big earthquake in the future and help teach Missourians how to prepare.

Today, Missouri is still growing and changing. More than six million people make their homes in Missouri. About 12 percent of people living in Missouri are Black. One of the fastest-growing groups is people of Hispanic and Latine descent, who make up about 5 percent of Missouri's population. Less than 1 percent of the population are Indigenous people from the United States, including Alaska. The Otoe-Missouria Tribe, which gave the state its name, is now based in Oklahoma.

Located in the middle of the United States, Missouri is central to the country's businesses and transportation. Industry continues to be strong as they make products and provide health, financial, and tourism services. Missouri's crops feed the nation. Millions of tourists visit the cities and small towns for adventure, exploration, and entertainment. Missouri is still of central importance to the country's geography, culture, and history.

Missouri at a Glance

Jefferson City

Statehood: 1821

Nickname: The Show-Me State

Abbreviation: MO

State Motto: *Salus populi suprema lex esto* (Latin for "Let the good of the people be the supreme law")

State Tree: Flowering dogwood

State Animal: Missouri mule

Capital: Jefferson City

Size: 69,707 square miles

Population: Over 6 million

Famous People from Missouri: Maya Angelou (poet), George Washington Carver (inventor), Kate Spade (fashion designer), Harry S. Truman (US president)

State flag

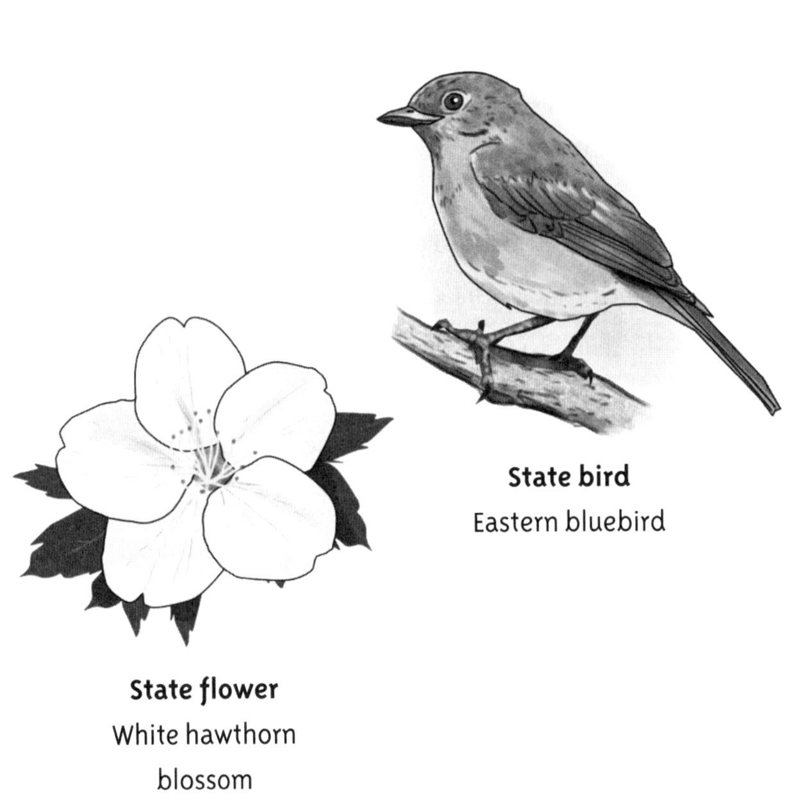

State bird
Eastern bluebird

State flower
White hawthorn blossom

FUN FACT:

The Missouri River is the longest river in the United States. From its source in the Rocky Mountains to St. Louis (where it meets the Mississippi River), it totals 2,540 miles.

Timeline of Missouri

900–1600 CE	The Mississippian people build settlements with mounds
1673	A group led by Louis Jolliet travels along the Missouri River and claims land for France
1750	French establish Ste. Geneviève
1803	The Louisiana Purchase doubles the size of the United States
1804	The Lewis and Clark Expedition begins in St. Louis
1821	The United States accepts Missouri as the twenty-fourth state
1857	The Dred Scott case is argued before the US Supreme Court
1860	The Pony Express begins in St. Joseph
1904	St. Louis hosts the World's Fair and Summer Olympics
1929	Many people lose jobs and money due to the Great Depression
1965	The St. Louis Gateway Arch is completed
1997	The first Build-A-Bear Workshop opens in St. Louis
2023	Kansas City Chiefs win the Superbowl
2024	Over one hundred tornadoes hit Missouri

Timeline of the World

1000 CE	Norse explorer Leif Erickson reaches North America
1607	Jamestown is founded in the colony of Virginia
1643	Louis XIV becomes King of France
1703	Russian ruler Peter the Great founds the city of Saint Petersburg
1783	The Montgolfier brothers fly the world's first hot-air balloon in France
1803	The Great Fire of 1803 burns in Bombay, India
1876	Alexander Graham Bell makes the first phone call
1914	The Panama Canal is completed, connecting the Atlantic and Pacific Oceans
1928	Mickey Mouse appears in Hollywood for the first time
1969	Neil Armstrong is the first person to walk on the moon
1992	The World Wide Web becomes available to the public
2020	The COVID-19 virus becomes a global pandemic
2024	About 15,000 athletes compete in the Summer Olympics and Paralympics hosted in Paris, France

Bibliography

***Books for young readers**

DeLano, Patti. ***Missouri: Off the Beaten Path***. Lanham, MD: Globe Pequot, 2024.

*Fradin, Judith Bloom and Fradin, Dennis Brindell. ***Who Was Sacagawea?*** New York: Penguin Workshop, 2002.

"Missouri." ***Britannica Kids***. kids.britannica.com/kids/article/Missouri/345501

"Missouri State Symbols." Missouri Secretary of State. sos.mo.gov/symbols

*St. George, Judith. ***What Was the Lewis and Clark Expedition?*** New York: Penguin Workshop, 2014.

Websites

Legends of America: legendsofamerica.com

Missouri Encyclopedia: missouriencyclopedia.org

Missouri State Parks: mostateparks.com

Official Missouri State Website: mo.gov

The State Historical Society of Missouri: shsmo.org

Visit Missouri: visitmo.com